Simply Charming Kids
Table of Contents

Moose on the Porch Quilts
Konda Luckau
665 E 400 S, Payson, UT 84651
kluckau@moosequilts.com
www.moosequilts.com

Introduction:

While writing the pattern book *Simply Charming*, I continued coming up with ideas for quilt patterns with charm squares. It turns out that I have not ended my love affair with charm packs. I love to pick up a charm pack and flip through it looking at the fabric, feeling the fabric, smelling the fabric and dreaming about making quilts from these little squares.

As a mother of 6 kids, an aunt to 30 kids (including three on the way), and the friend of people with kids, I make quilts for lots of kids. I enjoy making quilts for kids. I like to think that the quilts I make for them will be spit up on, carried around, and most importantly wrapped around these precious little (and not so little) ones. In order to facilitate the spitting and carrying and wrapping, the quilts in this book are simple, fast patterns. All of the patterns are great for beginners. In fact, these would be fun patterns to start a young quilter on.

Grab your favorite fabrics and start sewing! These versatile quilt patterns will look fabulous in any color way you are drawn to. Try one today!

Commonly Asked Questions about Charm Packs:

1) What is a charm pack?
A charm pack is a package of pre cut 5" squares. Generally a charm pack contains between 30 and 40 squares. All of the fabrics are different because the package includes one square of each fabric in a fabric line, excluding panels. Some fabric lines have one charm pack that contains the prints of the line and a separate charm pack that contains the woven fabrics which are commonly plaids of a particular line. Currently one fabric line puts two of each fabric in their charm packs making those quite a bit larger. Also, pre-measure your charm pack because currently one fabric line cuts their packs at $5\frac{1}{2}$" instead of the regular 5." This will not make a difference when making half square triangles, but it will make a difference when just using the squares.

2) Where can I buy charm packs?
Most quilt shops carry charm packs. They are also available online. Right now not all fabric manufacturers make charm packs, but more manufacturers will make them as everyone discovers how much fun they are!

3) What can I do with just one charm pack?
Some of the quilts in this book can be made with just one charm pack. Most of them can be made with just one charm pack if you forgo the charm square border. Depending on the size of the quilt you want to make and how many charms squares are in each package, you may want two or three charm packs.

4) What if my charm pack doesn't have enough squares in it?
Because the number of fabrics varies in each charm pack, it is impossible to tell the number of charm packs that each pattern will need. If a charm pack is lacking just a few squares, you have a couple options. First, you can always buy another charm pack and use the leftovers to make another quilt that doesn't take as many charms. Second, you can buy a fat quarter or two to get the extra fabric that you need. Another thing I have done, is purchase a little extra fabric for the borders or binding and cut a couple 5" squares out of the extra yardage.

5) Can I make these patterns without using charm packs?

Absolutely! Here are some places to find 5" squares:

~ Cut 5" squares out of your *scraps*. All of these quilt patterns make fabulous scrap quilts.

~ Cut 5" squares out of *yardage*. When purchasing yardage for 5" squares, 1/3 yard is a good amount to buy. That will give you two 5" strips with just 2" leftover. These 5" strips can each be cut into 8 squares so 1/3 yard of fabric will give you 16 charm squares.

~ Cut 5" squares out of a *fat quarter*. You can cut twelve 5" squares out of one fat quarter with a couple inches leftover.

~~~ All the patterns in this book are Fat Quarter Friendly!

6) Why should I buy a charm pack?

Here are my top ten reasons to buy charm packs:

1) They are just so fun!
2) To quickly achieve a scrappy look.
3) All the fabrics match.
4) You get a piece of an entire fabric line.
5) The squares are already cut.
6) To say, "Thank you!"
7) To say, "Happy Birthday!"
8) To say, "Merry Christmas."
9) They are quicker gifts than making cookies, less fattening, and last longer.
10) To be adventurous!

The reason I picked up my first charm pack was to be adventurous and stretch myself. I rarely buy plaids or grayed fabrics, but I love the comfortable look of quilts made using these fabrics. I decided to challenge myself to make a plaid quilt. I had a terrible time trying to select these fabrics. I fell in love with all the new brown fabrics that had come out, but I still couldn't get to the plaids. I wasn't brave enough to buy fabric I didn't absolutely love.

That was when I purchased a few of *Moda's Chocolat Wovens Charm Packs*. The result was *Simply Twisted,* which is in *Simply Charming,* and I was hooked! I love that quilt, and I never would have made it if I had to buy the fabrics one at a time. My hand would have passed over at least half of the fabrics.

For me, charm packs are mini-kits. Someone has put together 30-40 fabrics that look fabulous with each other. Occasionally in a charm pack, there are one or two fabrics that I really don't like. I will usually force myself to sew it into the quilt. Many times I find myself surprised that I like the offending fabric just fine once the quilt is finished because of the dimension and depth it adds to the quilt. Other times, I still don't like it, but there are only one or two in the quilt, so I am not disappointed with the overall result. And often I find that the fabric that I thought was so offensive is exactly the fabric that another person loves. That's part of the fun of quilting!

Good luck! I hope you have as much fun with these patterns as I have had making them.
Thanks, Konda Luckau

Square Dance
47" x 47"
16" block (15½" finished)

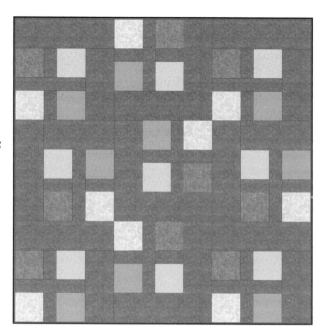

This quilt is made using an off balanced sashed four patch block. Rotating the block makes it look like it is dancing across the quilt. The throw size on page 13 is made with Chocolat by 3 Sisters for Moda. The twin size on page 14 is made with Gypsy Rose by Fig Tree Quilts for Moda.

Instructions are given for the Throw Size.

Fabric Requirements:
  36 charm (5") squares
  1⅔ yards for background
  2¼ yards for backing
  ½ yard for binding

Cutting Instructions:
1) Cut background fabric into the following strips:

	Baby Size	Throw	Twin Size	Queen Size
a) 5" strips	4 strips	**8 strips**	17 strips	30 strips
1) 5" x 16"	2 strips cut 4	**5 strips cut 9**	10 strips cut 20	18 strips cut 36
2) 5" x 11½"	2 strips cut 4	**3 strips cut 9**	7 strips cut 20	12 strips cut 36
b) 2½" strips	2 strips	**6 strips**	12 strips	21 strips
1) 2½" x 11½"	1 strip cut 4*	**3 strips cut 9**	7 strips cut 20	12 strips cut 36
2) 2½" x 5"	1 strip cut 8	**3 strips cut 18**	5 strips cut 40	9 strips cut 72

Sewing Instructions:
1) Randomly take 18 of the 5" charm squares and sew them onto 18 -- 2½" x 5" sashing strip as shown in **Figure A**.

Figure A

2) Randomly take remaining 18 -- 5" charm squares and sew them onto the other side of the sashing strip making 18 rectangle units as shown in **Figure B**. Press away from the sashing strip.

Figure B

3) Take the 9 -- 2½" x 11½" strips. Sew each of them in between two rectangle

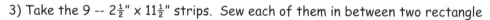

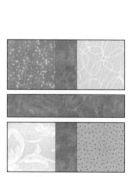

Figure C

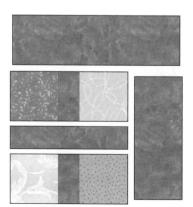

Figure D

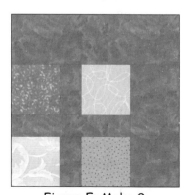

Figure E: Make 9

3   *There is extra fabric from Cutting Instruction a2 to cut one of the 2½" x 11½" rectangles.

units to make two four patch units as shown in **Figure C**. Press away from the sashing strip.

4) Take all of the 5" x 11½" strips. Sew one onto the right side of each of the nine four patch units as shown in **Figure D**. Press.

5) Take the 5" x 16" strips. Sew one onto the top of each of the blocks as shown in **Figure E**. Now there are 9 finished blocks.

6) Lay out your quilt rotating the blocks as shown in **Figure F: Assembly Diagram** for the throw size quilt or **Figure G: Assembly Diagram** for the Twin size quilt.

7) Sew the blocks into rows. Then sew the rows together. The throw size quilt should measure 47" x 47." The twin size quilt should measure 62½" x 78."

8) Refer to Appendix B Method 1 to cut and sew the backing fabric.

9) Quilt as desired.

10) Cut 5 -- 2½" strips width of fabric for the binding.

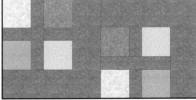

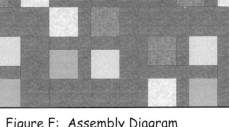

Figure F: Assembly Diagram
Throw Size

Figure G: Assembly Diagram
Twin Size

Alternate Size Chart for Square Dance

	Baby Size	Throw	Twin Size	Queen Size
Dimensions	31½" x 31½"	47" x 47"	62½" x 78"	93½" x 93½"
Layout	2 x 2	3 x 3	4 x 5	6 x 6
Charm Squares	16	36	80	144
Background	1 yard	1⅔ yard	3¼ yards	4¼ yards
Backing	1 yard	2¼ yards	4 yards	7½ yards
Binding	½ yard	½ yard	⅔ yard	1 yard

At a Crossroads
41½" x 50"
9" block (8½" finished)

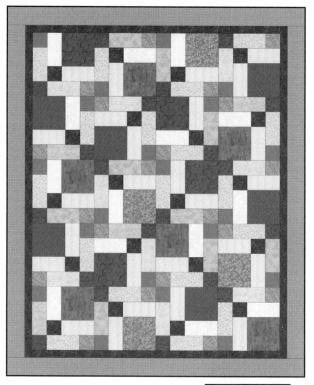

The split nine patch block was the inspiration for this quilt. I wanted to see what would happen if I took the idea a little further. Similar methods of construction are used that make this block fun to make. I think this block would make a fun mystery quilt because it may not make much sense in the middle of it. Stick with it, and you will be surprised at how fun it turns out!

The baby size quilt on the back cover was made using Wheels fabric by My Mind's Eye for Riley Blake Designs. The twin size quilt also on the back cover was made using Blush by Basic Grey for Moda.

Instructions are given for the baby size quilt.

Fabric Requirements:
  80 charm (5") squares
  ⅓ yard for the inner border
  ⅔ yard for the outer border
  2 yards fabric for backing
  ½ yard fabric for binding

Make 20

Cutting Instructions:
1) Separate the 5" charm squares into the following:

	Baby Size	Throw	Twin Size	Queen Size
# light charms	40	60	80	128
2½" x 5"	10 charms cut 20	15 charms cut 30	20 charms cut 40	32 charms cut 64
# medium charms	20	30	40	64
# dark charms	20	30	40	64
2½" x 5"	10 charms cut 20	15 charms cut 30	20 charms cut 40	32 charms cut 64

2) Cut the inner border fabric into 5 --1½" strips the width of the fabric.
     a) For either size, cut 1 of these strips in half.
3) Cut the outer border fabric into 6 -- 3" strips the width of the fabric.
     a) For the baby size quilt, cut two strips in half.

Sewing Instructions:
1) Take the 20 dark 2½" x 5" rectangles and the 10 of the light 5" charm squares. Sew one dark rectangle on both sides of a light square as shown in **Figure A**.

2) Press towards the dark rectangle. Cut all of these in half horizontally as shown in **Figure B** so you have 20 UNIT A rectangles that measure 2½" x 9" as shown in **Figure C**.

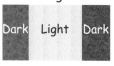

Figure A

Figure B

Figure C:
Make 20

3) Take the 10 dark 5″ squares and the 20 light 5″ squares. Sew one light square on both sides of a dark square as shown in **Figure D**.

4) Press towards the dark rectangle. Cut all of these in half horizontally AND vertically as shown in **Figure E** so you have 40 UNIT B rectangles that measure 2½″ x 7″ as shown in **Figure F**.

Figure D

Figure E

Figure F:
Make 40

5) Take 1 UNIT A rectangle, 2 UNIT B rectangles, 1 -- 2½″ x 5″ light rectangle, and 1 medium 5″ square to assemble one block as shown in **Figure G: Block Layout**. Repeat to make 20 blocks.

   1) Sew the light 2½″ x 5″ rectangle to the medium 5″ square to make one center unit. Press toward the medium 5″ square.

   2) Sew one UNIT B rectangle onto the bottom of one center unit. Press toward the medium 5″ square.

   3) Sew a second UNIT B rectangle onto the right side of the block. Press toward the medium 5″ square.

   4) Sew one UNIT A rectangle onto the bottom of the block. Press toward the medium 5″ square. The block should now measure 9.″

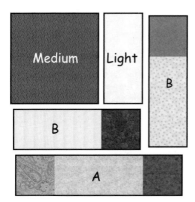

Figure G: Block Layout
Make 20

6) Lay out quilt center rotating blocks as shown in **Figure H: Assembly Diagram** for the throw size quilt and **Figure I: Assembly Diagram** for the twin size quilt.

7) Assemble the quilt center. Press. The quilt should now measure 34½″ x 43.″

8) Refer to Appendix A for tips on sewing on borders.

9) Take the 2 half 1½″ inner border strips. Sew each of them onto a whole 1½″ first border strip. First sew these strips onto the left side and the right side of the quilt. Then sew one of the whole strips onto the top of the quilt and the last whole strip onto the bottom of the quilt. Press.

10) Take four half 3″ outer border strips. Sew each of them onto a whole 3″ inner border strip. First sew these strips onto the left side and the right side of the quilt. Then sew one onto the top of the quilt and the last one onto the bottom of the quilt. Press.

11) Refer to Appendix B Method 1 to cut and sew the backing fabric.

12) Quilt as desired.

13) Cut 5 -- 2½″ strips width of fabric for the binding.

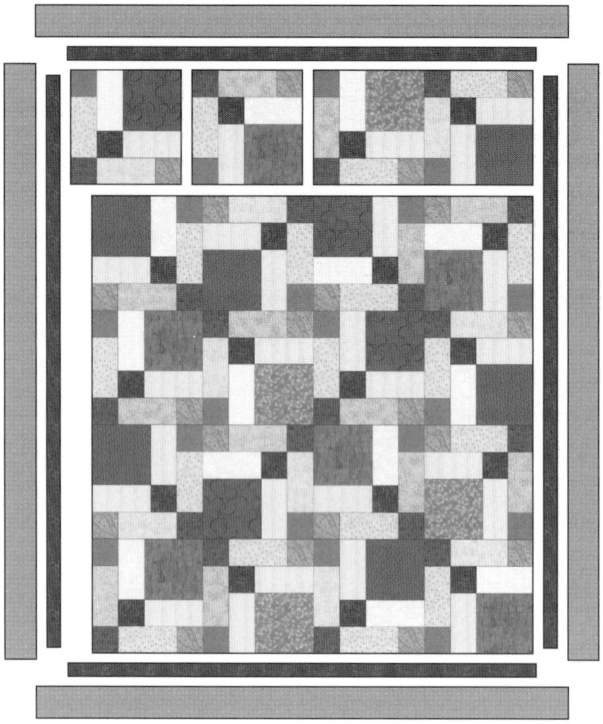

Figure H: Assembly Diagram
Baby Size

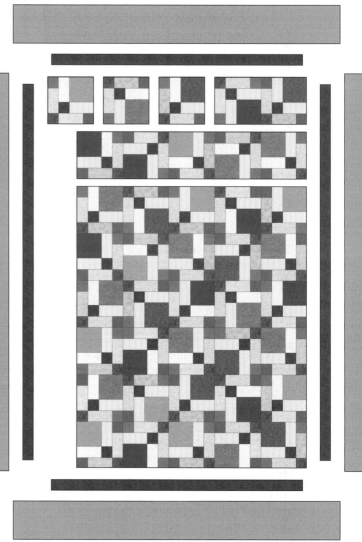

Figure I: Assembly Diagram
Twin Size

Alternate Size Chart for At a Crossroads

	Baby Size	Throw	Twin Size	Queen Size
Dimensions	41½" x 50"	52" x 60½"	61" x 86½"	91" x 91"
Layout	4 x 5	5 x 6	5 x 8	8 x 8
Charm Squares	80	120	160	256
1st Border	1½", ⅓ yard	1½", ⅓ yard	2½", ⅔ yard	3½", 1 yard
2nd Border	3", ⅔ yard	4", ¾ yard	7½", 2 yards	9", 2½ yard
Backing	2 yards	3½ yards	5 yards	7½ yards
Binding	½ yard	⅔ yard	¾ yard	1 yard

Rockin' Around the Block
53" x 53"
18" block (17½" finished)

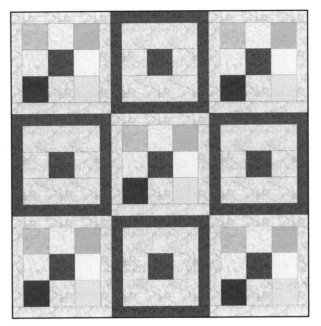

When I was 8½ months pregnant anxiously awaiting my daughter's arrival, I decided I needed to make her a quilt. I didn't have much time so it needed to be a quick pattern. I came up with Rockin' Around the Blocks. It was so fast I was able to get it done with time to spare!

The baby size quilt on page 16 was made using Hope Valley fabric by Denyse Schmidt for Free Spirit. The twin size quilt on page 17 was made using Martinique by 3 Sisters for Moda.

Instructions are given for the throw size quilt.

Fabric Requirements:
  40 charm (5") squares
  1⅔ yards for background
  1 yard for block centers and dark block border
  2½ yards for backing
  ½ yard for binding

Cutting Instructions:
1) Cut the background fabric into the following strips the width of the fabric:

	Baby Size	Throw	Twin Size	Queen Size
a) 5" strips	2 strips	4 strips	7 strips	12 strips
1) 5" squares	cut 4*	cut 8*	cut 14*	cut 24*
2) 5" x 14"	cut 4*	cut 8*	cut 14*	cut 24*
b) 2½" strips	4 strips	10 strips	16 strips	26 strips
1) 2½" x 14"	2 strips cut 4	5 strips cut 10	8 strips cut 16	13 strips cut 26
2) 2½" x 18"	2 strips cut 4	5 strips cut 10	8 strips cut 16	13 strips cut 26

2) Cut the block centers and dark block border fabric into the following strips width of fabric:

	Baby Size	Throw	Twin Size	Queen Size
a) 5" strips	1 strip	2 strips	2 strips	4 strips
1) 5" squares	1 strip cut 4	2 strips cut 9	2 strips cut 15	4 strips cut 25
b) 2½" strips	4 strips	8 strips	14 strips	24 strips
1) 2½" x 14"	2 strips cut 4	4 strips cut 8	7 strips cut 14	12 strips cut 24
2) 2½" x 18"	2 strips cut 4	4 strips cut 8	7 strips cut 14	12 strips cut 24

*From each 5" strip, cut 2 -- 5" squares and 2 -- 5" x 14" rectangles.

Sewing Instructions:

1) Take all 40 of the 5" charm squares and 5 of the block center squares. Use 8 of the charm squares and 1 block center and lay out in a Nine Patch Unit with the block center square in the center of the nine patch as shown in **Figure A**.

2) Sew blocks into rows. Press seams of the top and bottom row to the right and press the seams for the center row to the left. Sew rows together. Press. Repeat to make 5 Nine Patch Units.

2) Take all of the 2½" background strips for the border on the Nine Patch Units as shown in **Figure B**. First take 2 -- 2½" x 14" strips. Sew these onto the left side and right side of a Nine Patch Unit. Press toward the background strip. Repeat with all 5 Nine Patch Units.

3) Then take 2 -- 2½" x 18" strips. Sew these onto the top and bottom of a nine patch unit. Press toward the background strip. Repeat with all 5 Nine Patch Units.

4) Take the 8 -- 5" background squares and the 4 -- 5" block center squares. Sew a background square on both sides of each block center square to make 4 Center Units as shown in **Figure C**. Press.

5) Take the 8 -- 5" x 14" strips. Sew these strips on both sides of all 4 Center Units as shown in **Figure D**. Press.

6) Take all of the 2½" dark border strips for the border on the Bull's Eye Units as shown in **Figure E**. First take 2 -- 2½" x 14" strips. Sew these onto the left side and right side of a Bull's Eye Unit. Repeat with all 4 Bull's Eye Units. Press away from the border strip.

7) Then take 2 -- 2½" x 18" strips. Sew these onto the top and bottom of a bull's eye unit. Repeat with all 4 Bull's Eye Units. Press away from the border strip.

8) Lay out the quilt center as shown in **Figure F: Assembly Diagram** for the throw size quilt and **Figure G: Assembly Diagram** for the twin size quilt both on the following page.

9) Refer to Appendix B Method 1 to cut and sew the backing fabric.

10) Quilt as desired.

11) Cut 6 -- 2½" strips width of fabric for the binding.

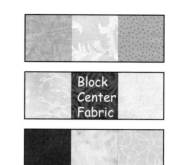

Figure A

Figure B:
Make 5 Nine Patch Blocks

Figure C

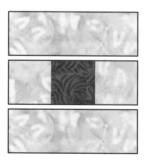

Figure D

Figure E:
Make 4 Bull's Eye Blocks

9

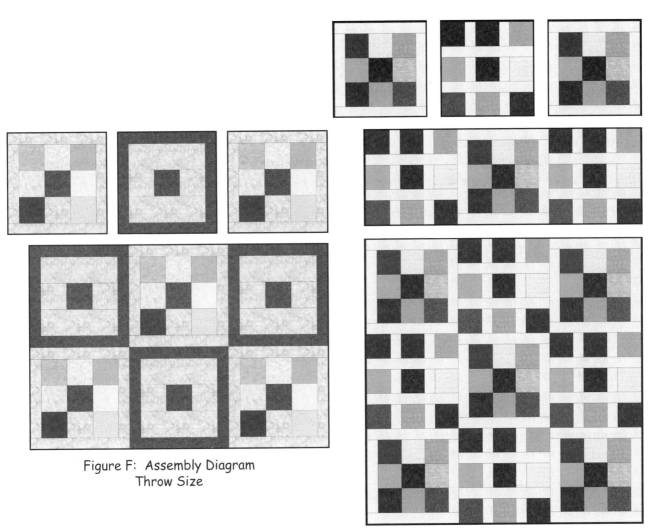

Figure F: Assembly Diagram
Throw Size

Figure G: Assembly Diagram
Twin Size

Alternate Size Chart for Rockin' Around the Block

	Baby Size	Throw	Twin Size	Queen Size
Dimensions	35½" × 35½"	53" × 53"	53" × 88"	88" × 88"
Layout	2 x 2	3 x 3	3 x 5	5 x 5
Charm Squares	16	40	64	104
Background	⅔ yard	1⅔ yards	2½ yards	4¼ yards
Dark Border	½ yard	1 yard	1½ yards	2½ yards
Backing	1¼ yards	2½ yards	4½ yards	7½ yards
Binding	½ yard	½ yard	⅔ yard	1 yard

Inside Out
41" x 53"
9 blocks
14" x 18" block
(13½" x 17½" finished)

I have enjoyed seeing rectangular shaped blocks recently. This quilt came about as I was thinking about how I would make a rectangular block out of charm squares.

The baby size quilt on page 12 was made using the Spring Fever fabric by Me & My Sister Designs for Moda. The twin size quilt on page 12 was made using Robots by David Walker for Free Spirit and others.

Instructions are given for the baby size quilt.

Fabric Requirements:
    44 charm (5") squares
    1 yard fabric for Block A border
    ⅔ yard fabric for Block B center
    2 yards fabric for backing
    ½ yard fabric for binding

Cutting Instructions:
1) Cut the fabric for the Block A border into the following strips the width of the fabric:

	Baby Size	Throw	Twin Size	Queen Size
a) 4¾" strips	3 strips	3 strips	7 strips	8 strips
1) 4¾" x 9½"	3 strips cut 10	3 strips cut 12	7 strips cut 26	8 strips cut 30
b) 2¾" strips	5 strips	6 strips	13 strips	15 strips
1) 2¾" x 18"	5 strips cut 10	6 strips cut 12	13 strips cut 26	15 strips cut 30

2) Cut the fabric for the Block B centers into 2 -- 10" strips the width of the fabric:

	Baby Size	Throw	Twin Size	Queen Size
a) 10" strips	2 strips	3 strips	6 strips	8 strips
1) 10" x 14"	2 strips cut 4	3 strips cut 6	6 strips cut 12	8 strips cut 15

Sewing Instructions:
1) Take 20 of the 5" charm squares. Make 5 Four Patch Units as shown in **Figure A**. Press.

2) Take the Four Patch Units and all 10 of the 4¾" x 9½" rectangles. Sew one of the rectangles to the top and another to the bottom of the Four Patch Units as shown in **Figure B**. Press toward the rectangle.

3) Take all 10 of the 2¾" x 18" rectangles. Sew one of the rectangles to the left side and another to the right side of the block as shown in **Figure B**.

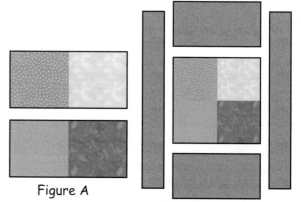

Figure A

Figure B: Make 5
Block A

Inside Out
Pattern on page 11
Pieced by Stacy Simmons
Quilted by Konda Luckau

Inside Out
Pattern on page 11
Pieced by Konda Luckau
Quilted by Konda Luckau

Square Dance
Pattern on page 3
Pieced by Konda Luckau
Quilted by Konda Luckau

Square Dance
Pattern on page 3
Pieced by Konda Luckau
Quilted by Konda Luckau

Building Blocks
Pattern on page 21
Pieced by Ashley Wheeler
Quilted by Konda Luckau

Building Blocks
Pattern on page 21
Pieced by Konda Luckau
Quilted by Konda Luckau

Rockin' Around the Block
Pattern on page 8
Pieced by Konda Luckau
Quilted by Konda Luckau

Rockin' Around the Block
Pattern on page 8
Pieced by Konda Luckau
Quilted by Konda Luckau

Reading Between the Lines
Pattern on page 25
Pieced by Konda Luckau
Quilted by Konda Luckau

Reading Between the Lines
Pattern on page 25
Pieced by Heidi Madson
Quilted by Konda Luckau

Press toward the rectangle. Now there are 5 of Block A. The block should measure 14" x 18."

4) Take the remaining 24 -- 5" charm squares. Randomly sew them together in sets of 3 as shown in **Figure C**. There should be 8 sets of three. Press.

5) Cut all 8 of these sets of three in half as shown in **Figure D**. This creates 16 Charm Strips that measure 2½" x 14."

6) Take all 4 of the 10" x 14" center rectangles and all of the Charm Strips to make Block B.

7) Take 1 center rectangle and 4 Charm Strips. Lay out one Block B as shown in **Figure E**. First sew a Charm Strip onto the left side of the center rectangle and another onto the right side of the center rectangle. Press toward the center. Repeat with all 4 center rectangles.

8) Next sew a Charm Strip onto the top and bottom of the center rectangle. Press toward the center. Repeat to make 4 of Block B as shown in **Figure E**. The block should measure 14" x 18."

9) Lay out the quilt as shown in **Figure F: Assembly Diagram** for the baby quilt and **Figure G: Assembly Diagram** for the twin size quilt on the following page.

10) Sew the blocks into rows. Press. Sew the rows together. Press.

11) Refer to Appendix B Method 1 to cut and sew the backing fabric.

12) Quilt as desired.

13) Cut 5 -- 2½" strips width of fabric for the binding.

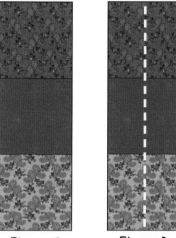

Figure C   Figure D

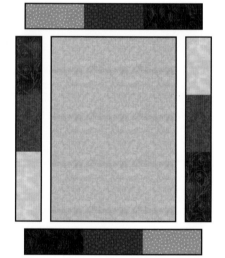

Figure E: Make 4
Block B

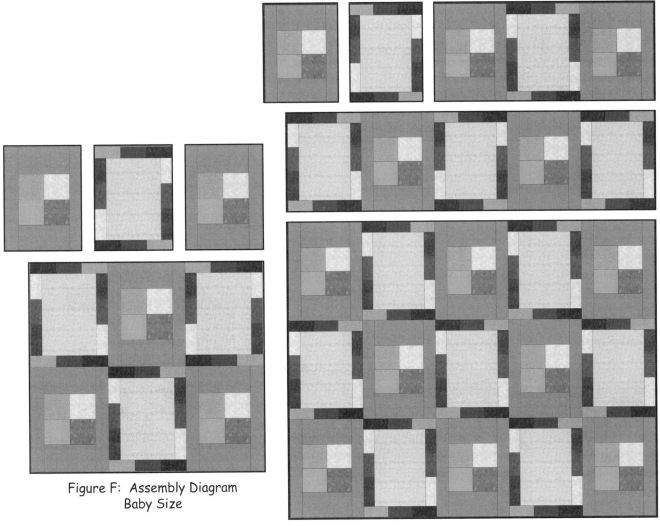

Figure F: Assembly Diagram
Baby Size

Figure G: Assembly Diagram
Twin Size

Alternate Size Chart for Inside Out

	Baby Size	Throw	Twin Size	Queen Size
Dimensions	41" x 53"	54" x 70"	68" x 88"	81" x 88"
Layout	3 x 3	4 x 4	5 x 5	6 x 5
Charm Squares	44	80	124	150
Block A Border	1 yard	$\frac{3}{4}$ yard	$2\frac{1}{8}$ yards	$1\frac{2}{3}$ yards
Block B Center	$\frac{2}{3}$ yard	$1\frac{1}{3}$ yards	2 yards	$2\frac{1}{2}$ yards
Backing	2 yards	3 yards	5 yards	$7\frac{1}{2}$ yards
Binding	$\frac{1}{2}$ yard	$\frac{2}{3}$ yard	$\frac{2}{3}$ yard	1 yard

Building Blocks
54½" x 54½"
18½" block (18" finished)

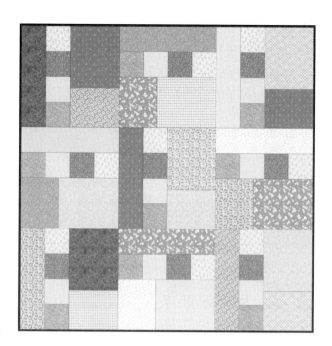

The block of *Building Blocks* was first published as *The Charming Path* in Simply Charming Two. It is a fun block that I have revised for this book. It is made from both fat quarters and charm packs. This is a quick quilt to put together because there are no matching seams in adjacent blocks. There is almost enough fabric left from the fat quarters to make a scrappy binding. If you choose this option, you will need a little more fabric to finish the binding.

The throw size quilt on page 15 was made using Deer Valley by Joel Dewberry for Free Spirit. The twin size quilt on page 15 was made using All Star Cottons by Riley Blake Designs.

Instructions are given for the throw size quilt.

Fabric Requirements:
    36 charm (5") squares
    9 fat quarters
    2½ yards for backing
    ½ yard for binding

Cutting Instructions:
1) Cut **all** fat quarters as shown in the **Figure A** as follows:
    a) Cut 1 -- 6" strip width of fabric
        Trim to 6" x 18½"
    b) Cut 1 -- 8½" strip width of fabric
        Cut strip into 1 -- 8½" x 7½" and 1 -- 8½" x 11½"
    c) (Optional) Cut 1 -- 2½" strip and set aside for the binding

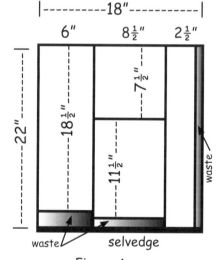

Figure A

Sewing Instructions:
1) Randomly sew together the charm squares into strips of 4 charm squares as shown in **Figure B**. Use all 36 charm squares to make 9 strips of charm squares. Press the seam allowances in one direction.

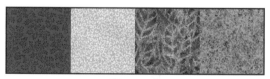

Figure B

2) Randomly take one of the 8½" x 7½" rectangles and one of the 8½" x 11½" rectangles and sew them together as shown in **Figure C**. Repeat with all 8½" x 7½" and 8½" x 11½" rectangles. There will be 9 of these rectangle units.

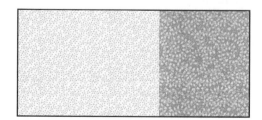

Figure C

3) Assemble blocks as shown in **Figure D**. Press seam allowances away from the charm squares.

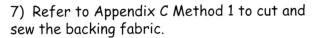

Figure D

4) Lay out the quilt rotating the blocks as shown in **Figure E: Assembly Diagram** for the baby quilt and **Figure F: Assembly Diagram** for the twin size quilt.

5) Sew blocks into rows.

6) Sew rows together. The throw quilt should measure 53½" x 53½" and the twin size quilt should measure 53½" x 88½."

7) Refer to Appendix C Method 1 to cut and sew the backing fabric.

8) Quilt as desired.

9) Cut 6 -- 2½" strips width of fabric for the binding or use the fat quarter strips for a scrappy binding adding more strips to the scrappy binding as needed.

 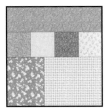 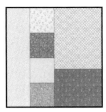

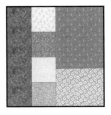 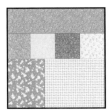 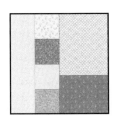

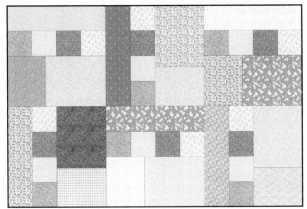

Figure E: Assembly Diagram
Throw Size

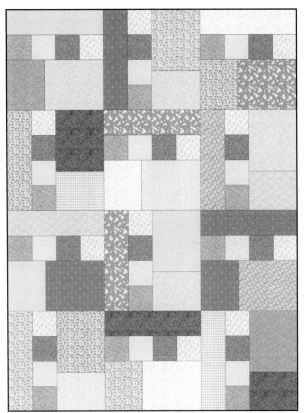

Figure F: Assembly Diagram
Twin Size

Alternate Size Chart for Building Blocks

	Baby Size	Throw	Twin Size	Queen Size
Dimensions	36" x 36"	54" x 54"	54" x 90"	90" x 90"
Layout	2 x 2	3 x 3	3 x 5	5 x 5
Charm Squares	16	36	60	100
Fat Quarters	4	9	15	25
Backing	1¼ yards	2½ yards	4½ yards	7½ yards
Binding	½ yard	½ yard	⅔ yard	1 yard

Times Square
53" x 53"
18" block (17½" finished)

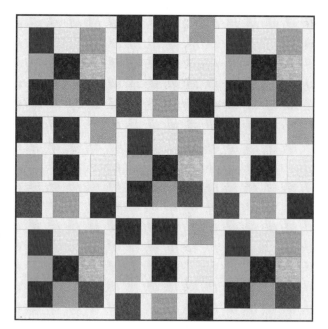

The nine patch block is one of my all time favorite blocks. It is so versatile. This quilt brings together a scrappy nine patch and a sashed nine patch which creates an interesting illusion.

The throw size quilt on the inside front cover was made using Animal Party by Amy Schimler for Robert Kaufman. The twin size quilt on the inside front cover was made using Eden by Lila Tueller for Moda.

Instructions are given for the throw size quilt.

Fabric Requirements:
- 81 charm (5") squares
- 1¼ yards for sashing
- 2½ yards for backing
- ½ yard for binding

Block A: Make 5   Block B: Make 4

Cutting Instructions:
1) Cut the sashing fabric into the following strips the width of the fabric:

	Baby Size	Throw	Twin Size	Queen Size
a) 2½" strips	8 strips	**17 strips**	29 strips	47 strips
1) 2½" x 5"	2 strips cut 12	**3 strips cut 24**	6 strips cut 42	9 strips cut 72
2) 2½" x 14"	2 strips cut 4	**5 strips cut 10**	8 strips cut 16	13 strips cut 26
3) 2½" x 18"	4 strips cut 8	**9 strips cut 18**	15 strips cut 30	25 strips cut 50

Sewing Instructions:
1) Take 45 of the 5" charm squares to use for Block A. Take 9 of these squares and lay them out in a nine patch unit as shown in **Figure A**. Sew together the nine patch unit. Repeat to make 5 nine patch units.

2) Take all 10 of the 2½" x 14" and 10 of the 2½" x 18" sashing strips to sew a border on the nine patch units as shown in **Figure B**.

3) First sew 2 -- 2½" x 14" strips onto the left and right side of a nine patch unit. Repeat with all 5 nine patch units. Press toward the border.

4) Then sew 2 -- 2½" x 18" strips onto the top and bottom of a nine patch unit. Repeat with all 5 nine patch units. Press toward the border. Now there are 5 of Block A.

5) Take the remaining 36 -- 5" charm squares and all 24 of the 2½" x 5" sashing rectangles. Now take 3 of the 5" squares and 2 of the sashing rectangles. Sew these together with the sashing rectangles between the charm squares as shown in **Figure C**. Press toward the charm squares.

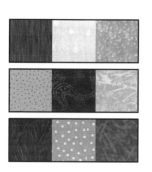

Figure A

Figure B: Make 5

Figure C

Repeat to make 12 sashed charm square units.

6) Take these Sashed Charm Square Units and the remaining 8 -- 2½" x 18" sashing strips. Take 3 Sashed Charm Square Units and 2 sashing strips. Sew these together with the sashing strips between the Sashed Charm Square Units as shown in Figure D. Press toward the sashing strip. Now there are 4 of Block B.

7) Lay out and assemble the quilt alternating Block A and Block B as shown in **Figure E: Assembly Diagram** for the throw size quilt and as shown in **Figure F: Assembly Diagram** for the twin size quilt. Press.

8) Refer to Appendix B Method 1 to cut and sew the backing fabric.

9) Quilt as desired.

10) Cut 6 -- 2½" strips width of fabric for the binding.

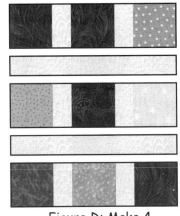

Figure D: Make 4

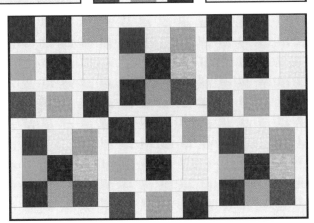

Figure E: Assembly Diagram
Throw Size

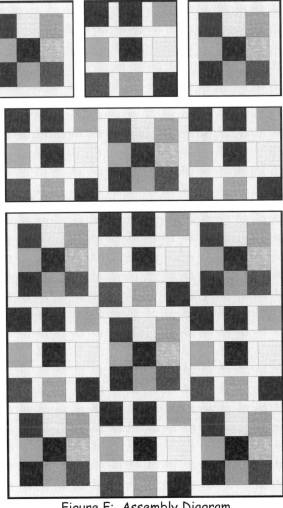

Figure F: Assembly Diagram
Twin Size

Alternate Size Chart for Times Square

	Baby Size	Throw	Twin Size	Queen Size
Dimensions	35½" x 35½"	53" x 53"	53" x 88"	88" x 88"
Layout	2 x 2	3 x 3	3 x 5	5 x 5
Charm Squares	36	81	135	225
Sashing	⅔ yard	1¼ yards	2¼ yards	3¼ yards
Backing	1¼ yards	2½ yards	4½ yards	7½ yards
Binding	½ yard	½ yard	⅔ yard	1 yard

Reading Between the Lines
47" x 47"
9 blocks
11½" block (11" finished)

This quilt came about as I was thinking about how to accent a background fabric. Contrast in the color and in the print of the fabric make a big difference in this quilt. Both of my samples have high contrast, but the pattern is less evident in Boogie Monsters because the patterns are so strong.

The throw size quilt on page 18 was made using Dance with Me by Jennifer Paganelli for Free Spirit and Hushabye by Tula Pink for Moda. The twin size quilt on page 18 was made using Boogie Monsters by Scott Jarrard for Free Spirit.

Instructions are given for the throw size quilt.

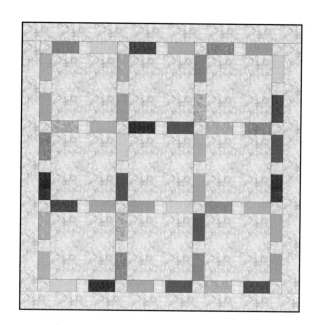

Fabric Requirements:
    24 charm (5") squares
    2 yards for blocks, sashing, and border
    2¼ yards backing
    ½ yard binding

Cutting Instructions:
1) From block, sashing, and border fabric, cut the following strips the width of the fabric:

	Baby Size	Throw	Twin Size	Queen Size
a) 2½" strips	2 strips	**3 strips**	5 strips	10 strips
1) 2½" x 5"	1 strip cut 6	**2 strips cut 12**	3 strips cut 19	6 strips cut 42
2) 2½" squares	1 strip cut 9	**1 strip cut 16**	2 strips cut 24	4 strips cut 49
b) 11½" strips	2 strips	**3 strips**	5 strips	12 strips
1) 11½" squares	2 strips cut 4	**3 strips cut 9**	5 strips cut 15	12 strips cut 36
c) border strips	cut 4 -- 3½" strips	**cut 6 -- 3½" strips**	cut 7 -- 6" strips	cut 9 -- 6" strips
		cut two in half	cut one in half	cut one in half

Sewing Instructions:
1) Take your 24 charm squares and the 12 -- 2½" x 5" rectangles. Sew a charm square on both sides of each rectangle as shown in **Figure A**. Make 12. Press toward charm squares.

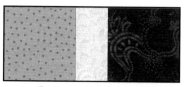

Figure A: Make 12

2) Cut in half lengthwise as shown in **Figure B**. Now there are 24 rectangle units that measure 2½" x 11½."

3) Lay out quilt as shown in **Figure C: Assembly Diagram**. First assemble each row. In the sashing strips, press seams toward the 2½" squares. In the block rows, press seams toward the 11½" block.

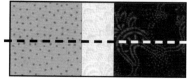

Figure B

4) Sew the rows together to finish assembling the quilt center. Press. The quilt should now measure 41½" x 41½."

5) Refer to Appendix A for instructions on sewing on border strips. Take the two half $3\frac{1}{2}$" border strips. Sew each one onto a whole strip. Sew one of these strips onto the left side of the quilt and another onto the right side of the quilt. Press.

6) Then sew one of these strips onto the top of the quilt and another onto the bottom of the quilt. Press.

7) Refer to Appendix B Method 1 to cut and sew the backing fabric.

8) Quilt as desired.

9) Cut 5 -- $2\frac{1}{2}$" strips width of fabric for the binding.

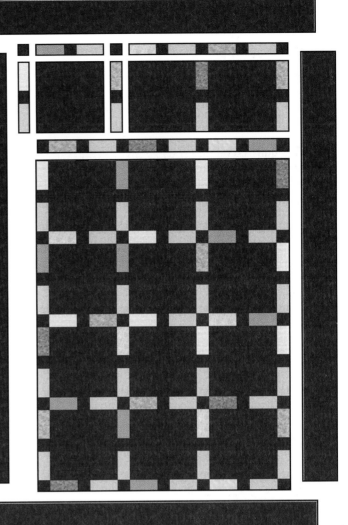

Figure D: Assembly Diagram
Twin Size

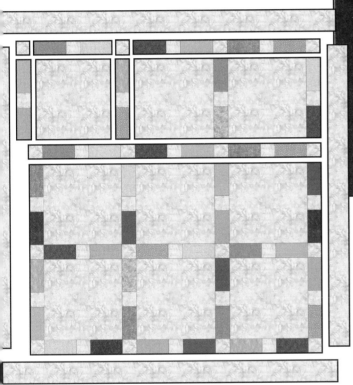

Figure C: Assembly Diagram
Throw Size

Alternate Size Chart for Reading Between the Lines

	Baby Size	Throw	Twin Size	Queen Size
Dimensions	35" x 35"	59" x 59"	53" x 79"	93" x 93"
Layout	2 x 2	3 x 3	3 x 5	6 x 6
Charm Squares	12	24	38	84
Blocks, Sashing, Border	$3\frac{1}{2}$" border, $1\frac{1}{3}$ yards	$3\frac{1}{2}$" border, 2 yards	6" border, $2\frac{1}{3}$ yards	6" border, $6\frac{1}{3}$ yards
Backing	$1\frac{1}{4}$ yards	$2\frac{1}{4}$ yards	$3\frac{1}{3}$ yards	$7\frac{1}{2}$ yards
Binding	$\frac{1}{2}$ yard	$\frac{1}{2}$ yard	$\frac{2}{3}$ yard	1 yard

Charming Churn Dash
48½" x 60½"
12 blocks
10½" block (10" finished)

The churn dash is a classic block that is one of my favorites. Also known as the monkey wrench, hole in the barn door, and many others, this was a fun block to make with charm squares.

The throw quilt on the inside back cover was made using Boutique by Chez Moi for Moda. The twin size quilt on the inside back cover was made from fat quarters. (Twelve charm squares can be cut from one fat quarter.)

Instructions are given for the throw quilt.

Fabric Requirements:
    36 charm (5") squares
    1 yard for background
    1 yard for sashing
    1 yard for border
    2¼ yards for backing
    ½ yard for binding

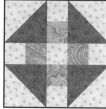

Make 12

Cutting Instructions:
1) Cut the background fabric into the following strips the width of the fabric:

	Baby Size	Throw	Twin Size	Queen Size
a) 5" strips	5 strips	5 strips	9 strips	14 strips
1) 5" squares	3 strips cut 24	3 strips cut 24	6 strips cut 48	9 strips cut 72
2) 2½" x 5"	2 strips cut 24	2 strips cut 24	3 strips cut 48	5 strips cut 72
b) 2½" strips	1 strip	1 strip	2 strips	3 strips
1) 2½" squares	1 strip cut 12	1 strip cut 12	2 strips cut 24	3 strips cut 36

2) Cut the sashing fabric into the following strips the width of the fabric:

b) 2½" strips	11 strips	11 strips	21 strips	28 strips
1) 2½" x 10½	3 strips cut 8	3 strips cut 8	6 strips cut 18	10 strips cut 30
2) Horizontal Sashing	3 strips	3 strips	8 strips	10 strips
3) Sashing Border	5 strips	5 strips	7 strips	8 strips

3) Cut the border fabric into 6 -- 5½" strips the width of the fabric.
    a) Cut 2 of these strips in half.

Sewing Instructions:

1) First organize your charm squares. Each block takes three charm squares -- two that are the same color and one that is a different color. As you are working with these squares, it will save time to keep them organized.

2) Take the 24 -- 5" background squares. Draw a diagonal line on the back of all of these squares.

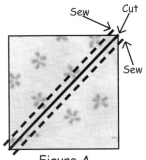

Figure A

3) Take all the sets of two matching charm squares from step 1 and all of the 5" background squares to create 48 half square triangles. To do this first take one charm square and one background square. Place them right sides together and sew ¼" on BOTH sides of the line as shown in **Figure A**.

4) Cut on the line. Press towards the charm square. Square up to 4½."

5) Repeat with all 24 background squares and all 24 charm squares to make 48 half square triangles as shown in **Figure B**.

Figure B

6) Take all 24 of the 2½" x 5" background rectangles and the remaining 12 charm squares. Sew a background rectangle on BOTH sides of each charm square as shown in **Figure C**. Press toward the charm square.

Figure C

7) Cut the unit in half vertically and horizontally as shown in **Figure D** so each unit becomes four 2½" x 4½" rectangles. There will be a total of 48 of these Rectangle Units.

8) Take 4 matching half square triangles, 4 matching Rectangle Units, and 1 -- 2½" background square. Lay out one block as shown in **Figure E**. Assemble block as shown. Press.

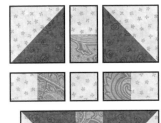

Figure D

9) Repeat to make 12 blocks.

10) Lay out the quilt as shown in **Figure F: Assembly Diagram** for the throw size and **Figure G: Layout Diagram** for the twin size.

11) First sew each vertical sashing strip onto the block to its left. Sew blocks and sashing together into rows.

12) Trim three sashing strips to 34½." Sew these sashing strips in between the rows of blocks. Then sew rows together. The quilt center should measure 34½" x 46½."

Figure E:
Make 12

13) Next sew on the sashed border. Refer to Appendix A for instructions on applying borders. Take the two half 2½" sashing strips and sew each of them onto a whole strip. Sew one of these strips onto the left side of the quilt and sew the other onto the right side of the quilt. Press.

14) Trim the last two 2½" sashing strips to 38½" long. Sew one onto the top of the quilt and the other onto the bottom of the quilt.

15) Now for the 5½" border. Take the four half 5½" strips, and sew each one onto a whole strip. Sew one of these long strips onto the left of the quilt. Sew another onto the right side of the quilt. Press.

16) Sew a third strip to the top of the quilt and the last strip onto the bottom of the quilt. Press.

17) Refer to Appendix B Method 1 to cut and sew the backing fabric.

18) Quilt as desired.

19) Cut 6 -- 2½" strips width of fabric for the binding.

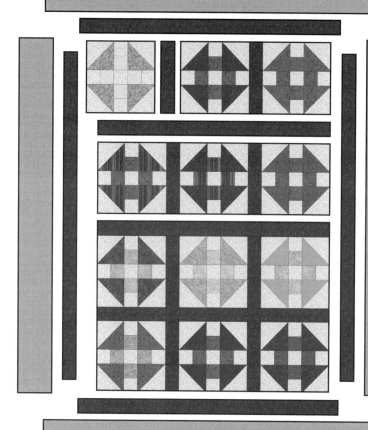

Figure F: Assembly Diagram
Throw Size

Figure G: Layout Diagram
Twin Size

Alternate Size Chart for Charming Churn Dash

	Baby Size	Throw	Twin Size	Queen Size
Dimensions	$38\frac{1}{2}$" x $50\frac{1}{2}$"	$48\frac{1}{2}$" x $60\frac{1}{2}$"	61" x 85"	91" x 91"
Layout	3 x 4	3 x 4	4 x 6	6 x 6
Charm Squares	36	36	72	108
Background	1 yard	1 yard	$1\frac{3}{4}$ yards	$2\frac{1}{2}$ yards
Sashing	1 yard	1 yard	$1\frac{2}{3}$ yards	$2\frac{1}{4}$ yards
Border	none	1 yard	$1\frac{1}{8}$ yards	$8\frac{1}{2}$", $2\frac{1}{3}$ yards
Backing	$1\frac{1}{2}$ yards	$2\frac{1}{4}$ yards	5 yards	$7\frac{1}{2}$ yards
Binding	$\frac{1}{2}$ yard	$\frac{1}{2}$ yard	$\frac{2}{3}$ yard	1 yard

Appendix A: Midge's Perfect Borders and Sashing

Care must be taken when sewing on long pieces of fabric. This method of applying sashing and borders is perfect for the beginning (and experienced) quilter. Using this method will ensure sashing and border lay flat. They will not be too tight leaving a "pregnant" quilt, and they will not be too loose leaving borders that ripple and wave. What it does not do is ensure that a quilt is square. This method maintains the shape of the interior of the quilt. So if your blocks and rows are square and pressed neatly, this method will preserve those square angles and your entire quilt will remain square. The sewing instructions will be given for applying borders. This method also works for sewing on long sashing strips.

Preparation:

1) Press everything neatly. Press blocks that sashing will be applied to and press the entire quilt that borders will be applied to.

2) Make sure the sashing or border strips are a little longer than the blocks or quilt they are being applied to and that they are also free of creases.

3) The only tools you need are pins. Have plenty on hand.

Sewing Instructions:

1) Stand up. First we will pin the left border. Line up the top left corner of the quilt and the end of the first border strip right sides together. Pin.

2) Hold the pinned area and gently shake the quilt and the border. This allows gravity to help line up the quilt and border for a few more inches. Pin. Take care not to stretch either the quilt or the border. Continue down the border by holding the next pin, shaking out, lining up the quilt and border, and placing the next pin. Pin approximately every 8".

3) After the border is pinned, trim the border even with the end of the quilt. Take care to make this cut straight and square to prevent "dog-eared" corners.

4) Sew on border with a $\frac{1}{4}$" seam allowance. Take care not to stretch either the quilt or the border. Holding onto the pins while sewing will prevent uneven stretching. Press.

5) Repeat with the right border and then with the top and bottom borders. Generally borders are applied in this order:
>   1) left and right inside borders
>   2) top and bottom inside borders
>   3) left and right outside borders
>   4) top and bottom outside borders

If there are more borders, they are added in the same order with left and right borders generally added before top and bottom borders.

6) Viola! A few pins and standing up to let gravity help makes quick work out of long unruly borders and sashing strips.

Appendix B: Piecing a Back

Many quilt shops carry backing fabric that is 90" wide or 108" wide which is handy because it eliminates the need to piece a back for the quilt. This fabric is usually very reasonably priced. However, for many reasons, quilters often need to seam fabric together to make a back large enough for the back of a quilt.

First, when figuring out how to seam a back, be sure the back is several inches larger both in the length and the width than the quilt top. If the quilt is 40" (sometimes 42") wide or smaller, then one length of fabric will be enough. The following examples apply when the width is greater than 40". Then we need to take the length into consideration when deciding how to piece the back together.

1) Length of the quilt is between 40" and 60"
~Take the width of the fabric and round up to a nice number. That is the whole length. To find the rest of the fabric needed, take half of that amount and add it to the whole length. That is how much fabric needs to be purchased.
~Cut the fabric into 2 pieces--one piece will be the "whole" length and the second piece will be the "half" length. Take the "half" length and cut it in half lengthwise. Lengthwise is the long side that is parallel to the selvedge. This cut will often be made on or close to the fold put in the fabric by the manufacturer.
~Sew the two short sides of this "half" length together so that now it is as long as the "whole" length. Sew onto the two lengths together as shown in Figure A.

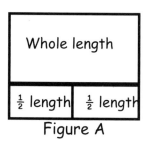
Figure A

2) Length of the quilt is between 60" and 80"
~Many quilts require this type of seaming. It is also the quickest.
~Take the width of the fabric and round up to a nice number. That is the whole length.
~Two lengths are needed so the amount is doubled. That is how much fabric needs to be purchased.
~Cut the fabric in half so there are two "whole" lengths. Sew the two lengths together along the selvedge as shown in Figure B.

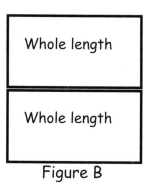
Figure B

3) Length of the quilt is between 80" and 100"
~Take the width of the fabric and round up to a nice number. That is the whole length. To find the rest of the fabric needed, take half of that amount and add it to TWO whole lengths. That is how much fabric needs to be purchased.
~Cut the fabric into two "whole" lengths and one "half" length.
~Take the "half" length and cut it in half lengthwise. Lengthwise is the long side that is parallel to the selvedge. This cut will often be made on or close to the fold put in the fabric by the manufacturer.
~Sew the two short sides of this "half" length together so that now it is as long as the "whole" length. Sew onto the three lengths together as shown in Figure C.

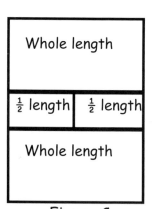
Figure C